52 Things Every Sales Manager Needs to Know

by Carl Henry

© 2008 Carl Henry. All rights reserved. Printed and Bound in the United States of America. No part of this book my be reproduced or transmitted in any form or by any means, electronic or mechanical, including photocopying, recording, or by an information storage and retrieval system – except by a reviewer who may quote brief passages in a review to be printed in a magazine, newspaper, or on the Web – without permission in writing from the author. For information, please contact Henry Associates, 9430 Valley Road, Charlotte, NC 28270.

Cover Design by Alex LaFasto
Book design by Nichole Ward, Morrison Alley Design

Although the author and publisher have made every effort to ensure the accuracy and completeness of information contained in this book, we assume no responsibility for errors, inaccuracies, omissions, or any inconsistency herein. Any slights of people, places, or organizations are unintentional.

First Printing 2008

ISBN 0-9657626-9-6

HELPING BUILD SALES LIBRARIES WORLDWIDE

Carl Henry
704-847-7390
www.carlhenry.com

Nancy

Sell Value Everyday!

Hope you enjoy "52 THINGS"

Carl

Introduction

If you want to learn something about sales management, there's no better place than the aisles of your local grocery store. In those rows, amongst the thousands of competing products, you'll find the good, the bad, and the ugly when it comes to the basics of packaging.

On the front of each box or can is a picture of the perfect meal – whether it's frozen lasagna or creamed corn, the photo suggests the very pinnacle of culinary delight. And what do we find next to these mouth-watering images? More promises, usually centered around how little fat there is in each bite, or how there isn't nearly as much salt as you'd expect. All of it creates a tidy little image: you're almost sitting down for a great meal, all you have to do is make the jump.

If you're ever distracted long enough to turn the item over, however, you'll find a different kind of label. This one won't have any appetizing photos, cartoon vitamins, or catchy slogans. In fact, it has nothing more than the government-mandated disclosure of the ingredients and nutritional content. While not nearly as flashy, these labels can be just as interesting on their own, especially when you find out your favorite snack is made from recycled tires.

The point here is that there are really two labels on every item – what you're being promised, and what's actually in the box. Marketers are usually hoping you won't notice the second label until you've already bought the product based on the first. And, in a way, I think sales management is a bit like that. Most managers come from a strong sales background themselves. They've figured out how to move product in the field, so they get promoted to help others do it. With that jump comes a salary hike, a bigger office, and a lot of new business cards with better embossing and an official title.

But, as most of you have learned by now, that's only what's on the front of the box. There's a lot more to being a manager than you saw as a salesperson. It isn't all meetings and sales trips to the islands. There are also late nights, stressful meetings with upper management, and letting good people go. Instead of managing your own client list, you now have to keep an eye on several or dozens of them. New problems creep up every day, usually with no easy solution.

In short, the picture on the box – the salary, the travel, and the prestige – isn't always what you're going to get, at least at first. In its place you've got a bunch of frozen ingredients, and you're going to have to work to make it taste good.

That's where I come in. Through my decades of work in sales – first as a successful salesperson and then as an author and trainer – I've seen what works and what doesn't. I've been to hundreds of annual meetings, thousands of internal gatherings. I've talked with CEOs, brand new sales trainees, and everyone in between. My work has taken me to industries as diverse as heavy machinery and real estate sales, to big companies and small ones, even across continents. In other words, I've been living and working like a traveling sales manager for a long time. What's more, I've gained a unique insight that can only come from being exposed to such a wide range of the industry. In these pages, I'm going to share that insight with you. I'm going to explain the back of the box and let you know what's good for you, along with what ingredients can harm your health.

Of course, if you've been working in sales or management for a while then some of what I say won't be new to you. In fact, I'd go as far as to say you'll have seen a few of these issues crop up many times over your career. So why repeat them now? Because they're that important. Like nutrition, it's easy for us to forget the fundamentals of sales and management on a day-to-day basis. After all, they aren't as tasty as bad habits are. But, if you want to really fly as a sales manager – and the rewards are wonderful – you're going to have to do the hard work every day, not just once in a while. Don't worry though, most of what you find won't just make sense, it will be fairly easy to put into motion.

Before we jump right into the tips, let me start by saying that sales management, like all kinds of management, really has two aspects. The first is mastery of the technical matters – knowing your product and the industry, learning the numbers and ratios in your business, and so on. It's nearly impossible to do a good job managing your team if you aren't sure how much it costs you to bring in a new customer, or how much your competitors charge for something similar to your flagship product. To that end, you'll notice that I stress the importance of these tools, along with ways for managers to improve their knowledge base.

But the second component is one that's far easier to grasp, and much harder to actually give – leadership. There's no substitute for your staff's belief in you. If you want them to sell, they need to trust you at the top. There can't be any question of your character or attitude. No matter what it says on your business card or office plate, you're going to have to show you're committed to doing the right things, not just saying them, and a number of the tips will reinforce this.

And, finally, as you read through these pages, remember that sales management is just like selling was. The longer you do it, and the more attention you pay, the better you're going to get over time. I've intentionally given you 52 pieces of advice – one for each week of the year. Focus on some aspect of your performance four or five days until it becomes second nature, then move on to the next one. Don't try to change everything at once; work on improving one small area at a time. Excellence hardly ever comes from one huge effort; it's much easier to cultivate with thousands of smaller ones.

Let's get started…

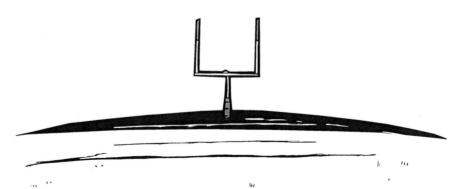

SALES ARE WON IN THE FIELD, SO THAT'S WHERE YOU HAVE TO MANAGE

1

Technology can do a lot of great things for you, but it can also make it easy to get lazy. Lots of managers make their way into a big office and then forget about all of the things they did to become successful. On the way up, they met every client and firmed up closes with handshakes. But when they need to find out what's going on with their sales staff, they resort to cell phones and emails.

This is a dangerous way to supervise a team. For one thing, it removes you from what's actually going on in the field. How can you know what your producers are up to if you never see them in action? Asking them for progress updates, without ever checking in personally, isn't enough. This is especially true for younger salespeople, who might not have enough knowledge or experience to explain where they are in a sale, or what their strengths and weaknesses are.

Staying in the office also puts you at another disadvantage by showing your producers you aren't willing to get your hands dirty. We all respect leaders who let us know they're willing to go where we go. Not only does it make them more genuine, but it gives a real basis for teaching and recommendations. Nobody wants to be critiqued by someone who's never seen their work.

Do yourself and your team a favor and get out into the field once in a while. A couple of quick trips can save you hundreds of hours in e-mails, phone calls and meetings. And that's not just efficient management – it's strong leadership.

52 Things Every Sales Manager Needs to Know

2

Vision is a popular topic. Politicians use it to talk about their plans for the future, CEO's tout it as a bridge to bigger profits, and even athletes mention it as a big part of their success. So, with all this attention being paid to vision already, why mention it here?

Because for all the overblown talk, vision – a focus on some possibility of the future, a sense of what could be over the horizon – is something every leader needs. And that's not just something you want to be thinking about; it's something that you'll want to cultivate in yourself and your staff.

So indulge in your vision. Live it in your mind, explore its depths and contours. But most of all, share it. Let your producers know what you see down the road, and how you want to get there.

Every sales activity, from prospecting to asking for the order, is a means to an end. What is it that you really want from those ends? Is it the most profitable company in your industry? The biggest market share? A huge bonus for everyone in the department? Whatever it is that you see in your mind's eye, express it to your staff and let them see their part in it. Show them how much you can feel it, and what will happen when you all reach the goal together.

Vision has been abused by so many people selling books, seminars and programs that it's almost lost all meaning. But that doesn't mean it isn't still a powerful and essential part of effective management.

A great sales manager has a great depth of knowledge

3

When you were hired or promoted to your sales management position, what did the job description look like? Chances are, it left out a few dozen of the tasks and skills you need to really succeed. The best managers I know aren't just supervisors. They're also part-time accountants, therapists, teachers, strategists, communicators and presenters – not to mention numerous other roles I've skipped over here.

So how do managers master all of these tasks? By cultivating a great depth of knowledge. In other words, they never stop learning. In my books and seminars, I've made a big deal of my belief that every salesperson should continue reading and absorbing anything that can help his or her career. Accordingly, I think managers should do whatever they can to encourage those habits. But telling your staff to keep studying isn't enough – you need to lead the charge. Not only will you reap all of the same benefits in your career and paycheck, but you'll show your sales team that you take what you're telling them seriously. Remember, there's no leadership technique as powerful or impacting as a good example.

A few years ago, at the conclusion of a presentation, one of my clients approached me and said something that I'll never forget. "Carl," he told me, "It's good to see someone who enjoys their craft so much." I think that one remark summed up a great deal of my success. I genuinely enjoy what I do, and so I make an effort to keep getting better at it. To succeed at sales in any level – whether it's selling, managing, or teaching – merely having a job isn't enough.

Be careful with special discounts. Use them too often, and they won't be very special to your customers anymore — but your regular prices will

4

Would you pay full sticker price for a new car? Probably not, because most of us know that no matter what time of year it is, a sale on autos is just around the corner. Dealers will take advantage of any holiday – or just make one up – to move inventory off the lot. So we take advantage by waiting until the savings show up.

Your customers are no different. If you're constantly tempting them with one price break or another, you condition them to wait for sales, and to never pay full price. Why should they, if they know they can wait a few weeks for a better deal? Worse yet, you teach your sales staff bad habits. Instead of encouraging them to build up value and learn to hold strong to their prices, you send the message that giving away margins is a good way to close customers.

With that in mind, take care not to overdo special pricing. Relay to your producers, not to mention executives and warehouse managers, that running too many sales is a losing strategy. And if you must advertise discounts, make sure that they're small and tied to a specific event that isn't based on the calendar – new products offerings, closeouts on inventory, and so on.

While there will certainly be times when a special deal or discount price is appropriate, don't get into the habit of running too many sales. It might be an easy way to increase revenue in the short term, but it won't be too long before you need a cowboy hat and a stack of rebates just to close a customer.

When it comes to your sales staff, be slow to hire and quick to fire

5

One of the biggest and most costly mistakes sales managers make is hiring everyone in sight and then holding on to them forever. While it might be easier than doing the hard work of finding top talent and weeding out the rest, it also leaves them with a team that will never grow and develop into top performers.

There are lots of people who aren't cut out for sales. And yet they enter the field, year after year, in every industry. Many of them are fresh graduates or career-changers who have never worked in sales before. They underestimate the amount of hard work it takes, or don't have the kind of self-motivating personalities that are needed to succeed. Others are simply looking for a job and know that sales positions are easy to come by. Whatever their reasons, it's critical that you weed out as many of them as possible. You simply cannot succeed as a manager if you don't hire effective salespeople.

On the other hand, when it becomes apparent that one of your new producers isn't going to work out, don't be slow to cut them loose. Many managers fail in this area and hold on to ineffective producers because they want to be kind, or don't want to admit a mistake. So they keep stragglers on the payroll, hoping they'll be able to mold them into better salespeople. But you're not doing anyone any favors by holding on to someone ill-suited for this particular career, and additional time and training are probably going to be wasted.

Take your time hiring the right people, and then quickly cut ties with those that don't work out. It might be difficult at first, but over time both you and your new hires will be rewarded with higher sales and lower turnover.

To grow a SUPERSTAR sales team, build a concept of continuing education

6

You probably wouldn't be in management if you weren't already a strong producer. And chances are, you didn't get to that level by taking in one sales seminar or listening to a couple of tapes. Most top-shelf salespeople I know got to where they were by constantly absorbing new information and honing their craft. Why not try to instill that same attitude into your staff?

On top of the many hats a sales manager has to wear every day – coach, motivator, negotiator, etc. – I'd like to add one more: educator. Whether you think of yourself as a tutor, professor, dean or teacher isn't important. What is important is that you impress upon your staff that you got to where you are by continually learning and refining your skills.

Don't stop with just telling them, either. Lead by example. If your team knows you set aside fifteen minutes a day to read a book on management, they might take up a similar habit. Make a point of attending a seminar once in a while, and they may take the hint that successful salespeople can't get stale.

Times change, but the need to keep getting better doesn't. For newer salespeople, learning and mastering the basics of sales can mean the difference between a great career and a short one. And for the rest of us, continuing education is a way to maintain our edge. Be sure your staff understands this, and that you don't forget it either.

If you want a happy sales team, don't mess with territories

or

COMMI$$IONS

7

One of the classic mistakes in sales management is one of the easiest to predict: messing around with your staff's territories or commissions. You'd think this would be obvious, and yet I see managers, even veterans, fall for it all the time. In an effort to get bigger numbers, bring up a new salesperson, or even out the pay-scale they decide to carve up an area or change the way people get paid.

On the surface, these might seem like good ideas. So why do I say this blunder is so predictable? Because it ignores a basic fact: good salespeople are motivated by money and the desire to stand out above the rest. And any time you start changing who they can sell to, or what they'll get paid for it, you're messing with those motivations. In other words, you're running the very real risk of taking away what's important to them; you're inviting them to stop working for you.

For example, I've seen situations where a top salesperson was making as much, or more, than the president of the company. Instead of seeing this as a signal that their superstar was doing a great job, upper management viewed it as a chance to cut back on the commission rate. In most cases, the salesperson either sells less or simply moves on to work for a competitor.

With that in mind, try to resist the urge to alter either one unless it's absolutely necessary. If you think you might have to make a switch, discuss it with your sales staff beforehand. They might surprise you – the fear of loss is a powerful thing, and I've seen salespeople work incredibly hard to hang on to their ground. And if you do have to change things up eventually, they'll know it was a reasoned decision, not a knee-jerk reaction.

YOU DON'T HAVE TO BE A MATHMETICIAN, BUT YOU HAD BETTER KNOW THE NUMBERS IN YOUR BUSINESS

8

There's an old saying that "numbers don't lie," and when it comes to sales, at least, I've found it to be true. When you were selling, you probably had a good idea of how many calls it took to generate an appointment, how many appointments you needed to make a presentation, and what your closing ratio was from there. As producers, these numbers will dictate, over time, how much money you'll make and what kind of career you'll have. They can do the same for managers.

Don't just show your sales team how to calculate the important numbers, keep track of them yourself as well. Are some of your producers making a lot of appointments but few actual sales? They might need work on asking for the order. Are they making too many sales at low margins? A refresher on negotiating might be in order. By keeping tabs on the ratios and percentages your staff is working with, you'll be able to spot problems and opportunities, as well as give more meaningful goals and advice.

Besides, learning the facts and figures isn't just good for sales – it's great career advice. Most sales managers strive to move up into executive leadership. It's a natural fit, since they know the products, the market, and how to reach the executives. But once you get to the board room, it's as much about balance sheets and return on investment as it is reading personalities and making deals. The manager with a good understanding of finance has a leg up. Do yourself and your sales team a favor; embrace the numbers side of your business. You might be surprised at how quickly it adds up.

Be easy on your salespeople, but take their problems head on

9

Somewhere along the way, good management got mixed up with stern lectures, sarcastic remarks and, occasionally, lots of yelling. For some supervisors, it seemed like a good way to show their staff "they meant business." For others, it was just a reflection of how they were brought up in the business. A lot of today's veterans, myself included, were brought up in offices where profane rants were like smoking – just part of the landscape.

These days, however, we know that neither habit does much good for us or the people with whom we work. And since I'm pretty sure you already work in a smoke-free office, I'm going to give you some good advice – be easy on people, but tough on problems.

What does this mean? It means that you should remember you're on the same side as your staff, and treat them accordingly. There are going to be some things with which your salespeople will have difficulty. But show your producers some respect, and work to develop them into top performers. Deal with their shortcomings like a teacher, not the leader of a chain gang. Don't fall into the habit of calling them lazy or incompetent. If either is really true, then you should replace them. Otherwise, hold your tongue and help out. It might be that they're struggling with their sales and just need a nudge in the right direction.

It's easy to think being tough on your staff is the only way to get them to learn things, especially if that's how you were brought up in the business. But by attacking their selling problems, rather than the individuals, you can become a much better teacher – and a richer manager.

The goal of training isn't more training — it's results

A client once told me that every time he hired me, his company's sales went up. It's hard for me to think of a better compliment or endorsement for what I do, but it also got me thinking. Why is it, I wondered, that so few managers think of their training decisions in that way? Why aren't they worried about getting the most bang for their buck?

Most of you wouldn't buy an expensive piece of equipment if you didn't expect it to pay for itself in increased output or efficiency. You wouldn't bring in a new salesperson without any thought to whether he or she will generate new business or not. And yet, I continually run into situations where the only "training" a company has done is bringing in a motivational speaker from time to time.

Motivation is an important part of sales, and one that you shouldn't skimp on, but it can't take the place of actual training. With that in mind, don't try to have someone pump up your staff and expect them to develop new skills overnight. To really improve performance, you need spaced interval training – that is, lessons reinforced over time. This basic technique, used by organizations from NASA to the NBA, is a lot simpler than its name suggests. You just teach someone something, let them practice it, and then come back to teach it again. The process starts when they become aware of what they're doing, and ends when they can do it consistently without even thinking about it.

Top performance is never a mystery or an accident. It's simply the natural result of lots of time and hard work. Remember that as you approach your training efforts. It's great to be entertained, but it's even better if it results in more sales.

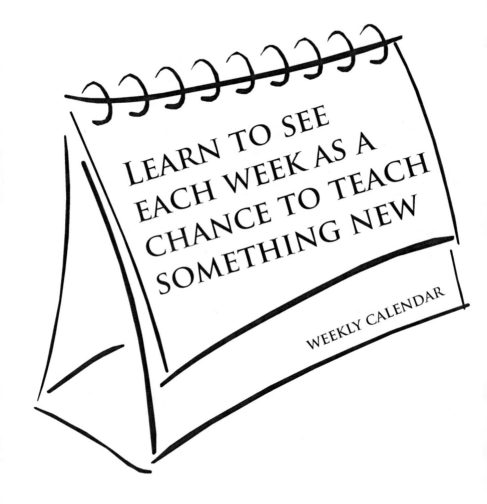

One of the best sales managers I know is from the South. While her company, a large consulting firm, is constantly adding and losing sales staff, she consistently has a roster full of top performers. Her secret? Using each week as a chance to teach and present something new to them.

Every Monday morning, she introduces her producers to something new they can work on throughout the week. On some occasions, it might be a specific tactic like gathering leads at a trade show. Other times, she might invite personnel from another department to talk about the features of a new product or service plan. Or, it might even be something general, like building more value into your sales, or holding on to prices. The point is, each week they have one thing they'll be concentrating their energy on exclusively. She introduces the topic with a quick talk, possibly followed by a one or two page handout, questions, and a quick activity. The whole thing only takes a few minutes, but it's paid huge dividends.

Not only does it help keep things fresh for the sales staff, but over the years it has reinforced key skills – like prospecting, using a sales system, negotiation, and so on – again and again. Her producers never fall into a rut, because they're always working on something different, sharpening their skills along the way.

This is an easy tactic any sales manager can use to fire up the staff and improve production. Don't go overboard and eat up more than a few moments a day, but take advantage of the time you have each week to teach something new. By the time Friday comes around, you'll have a stronger, fresher team.

If your top producer isn't a team player,

you have a problem

12

Successful salespeople almost always have healthy egos, and that's a good thing. Getting the biggest commissions often means raking through hours or even days of rejections; only the strongest personalities can keep coming back time and again. But sometimes this can go too far.

If you haven't experienced this as a manager, then you've probably at least seen it during your days as a salesperson: there is one producer doing more business than several others combined. Because of this, he or she starts to demand special treatment, and gets it. They represent such a big chunk of revenue that it would be foolish to upset them. But over time, their behavior becomes more erratic and self-centered; they insult personnel in other departments, or lower-performing sales people. Eventually, they may stop taking direction or start making larger demands, monetarily or otherwise.

The key to dealing with it is holding on to some balance. In a sense, the top producer is right – those people are special. They can do what most people can't, and they need a certain amount of arrogance to do it. On the other hand, you can't let them ruin morale in your department.

So the first step is to rein them in before they get too far out of bounds. Take care to recognize their achievements, but at the same time, don't let them run free of any supervision. Pay close attention to what your other producers or other departments have to say about them. If you sense you might have a problem, talk to them about it. And, no matter what, always keep recruiting top people and developing them within your organization. If you are forced to let a top salesperson go, things will be a lot easier if you have several others ready to take his or her place.

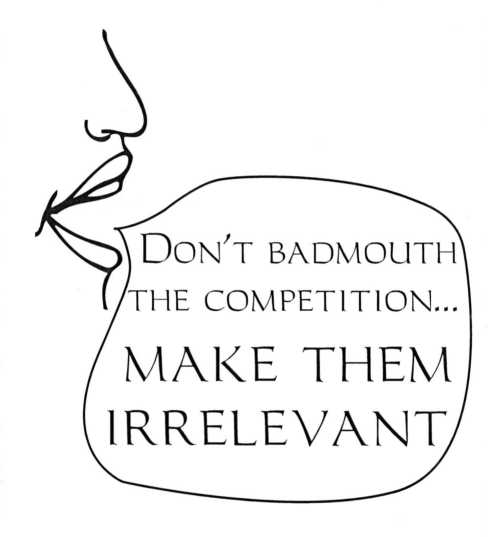

13

No matter what you sell, if you're making any money in it, then someone else is trying to sell it as well. In our world, there really aren't any competition-free industries left. That's not necessarily a bad thing – competitors can force us to stay sharp and focused – as long as we don't take our focus off of our own activities.

Make sure your sales staff knows about your competitors' products, and how they stack up against yours. Prepare literature that shows the advantages of your solutions, as well as price comparisons. Give your producers an idea of your relative histories and positions in the industry.

Beyond that, however, let it go. The challenge to your department is to sell your products, not to worry about what some other company is doing. And be sure your salespeople are taking that attitude with them out into the field. Don't let them fall for the trap of talking down a competitor or their products. It's unprofessional, and usually leaves the customer questioning your credibility instead of your competitor's. Instead, have them talk about areas where your company shines, and most of all, keep the discussion focused on building value for the customer.

When it comes down to it, the best way to deal with competitors is to outsell them. Because once you've built a leading position in your area or industry, you won't have to answer questions about competitors – you can leave that to the other guy.

14

Twenty years ago, hiring for sales was basically akin to rolling the dice. After digging through a small mountain of resumes and interviewing a handful of candidates, a manager would be forced to take a gamble on the few that seemed promising. Of those, most would wash out of the business completely, a few would hang on to become average performers, and every one in a hundred would break out to be a sales star.

In many industries, the numbers haven't improved that much, but not for lack of better tools. Researchers have gone to great pains to find out what makes a sales star, how they think, and where their motivations lie. And, with those pieces in place, they've developed detailed personality assessments – a kind of sales aptitude test. So why aren't more managers taking advantage? Your guess is as good as mine.

It amazes me, in this day and age, that anyone would think of hiring a salesperson without giving them an assessment first. For no more than a few dollars and a couple of hours, you can gain more information than you would in years of working with someone. Before you commit the time and money it takes to bring a new hire in, you want to know four things – which, coincidentally, are the exact four things an assessment can tell you – how they sell, why they sell, can they sell, and will they sell. Bringing someone in without that kind of data is an expensive gamble.

If you haven't been using assessments in your hiring decisions, I'd advise you to start doing so today. All you have to do is e-mail me at chenry@carlhenry.com, and I can set one up for you in a matter of minutes. Hiring is one of the most important parts of a sales manager's job – use the best tools to make the numbers work for you.

To understand your staff, understand yourself first

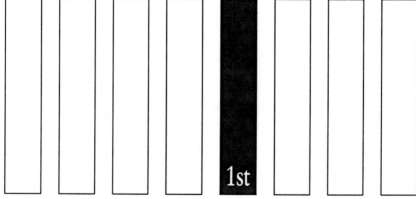

There's an old quote I love by Lao Tse: "He who knows others is learned; he who knows himself is wise." I don't know much about Lao beyond his fortune cookie wisdom, but I'd be willing to bet he would have made a strong sales manager. Even without the benefit of any seminars or sales manuals – which were harder to come by around sixth century BC – he grasped one of the most important tenets of the job.

Managing people effectively takes a lot of insight and strong communication skills. Like sales, it's largely a matter of identifying and feeding another person's motivations. I've seen in my own career how learning about different personality styles can translate into increased sales, and made it a corner of my own MODERN Sales System. But for managers, personality styles are even more important. This is because you don't have to just sell your staff once; you have to convince them to buy into your vision every day.

To do so, you'll need to understand where they are coming from, and more importantly, how they see you and relate to you. And you'll never be able to do that without a good understanding of your own personality style – your inherent tendencies and motivations.

You should know by now that I would advise you to never hire a salesperson without first performing a personality assessment. It's a small investment, and one that will shed a huge amount of light onto their chances for success. But as you try to understand personalities, don't overlook the one that might influence your team's success the most – your own. Take the time to assess yourself. What you find won't just be interesting, it will make you a better leader.

Productive sales managers strive to make their sales force self-sufficient

16

I've noticed over the years that poor managers are usually much busier than their more successful counterparts. Do you want to know why? Because they have a sales staff that comes to them for everything, whether it's a product detail, information on pricing, or just advice on closing a sale. Naturally, there are legitimate questions and concerns all managers should expect and deal with. But the problem arises when the sales staff doesn't take any of the initiative on themselves.

Like the parents of spoiled children, these managers often recognize they have a problem. And yet, just as predictably, most of them will blame their staff. The salespeople are just too lazy, they say, or unmotivated. That may be true, but guess what? They take their cues from the top.

Communicate clearly with your salespeople that you're there to support them, but you expect them to take care of small problems themselves. Root them in a strong sales system – like MODERN – so they'll know how to follow its steps; coach them on the best ways to find solutions and present them to customers; and then let them work. By continually offering more help than they need, you aren't just wasting your time; you're also undermining their confidence and teaching them to come to you for all the answers.

Top producers rarely need a lot of management or guidance. Your goal should be to have all of your sales staff reach that level, so they'll only need your input on important issues. Reach that point and you won't just have more time and more money; you'll have given yourself a much easier job.

A solid sales system is the foundation of a successful sales team

17

When I first developed The MODERN Sales System, it wasn't because I was dying to write a book or teach seminars. In fact, my motivation was simple – I still didn't understand the selling process well enough. Put another way, I didn't always know what I should be doing with my customers, and when.

In studying sales, though, I came to a simple truth. Every sale is a predictable process. It has a beginning, a middle, and an end. The easiest way to ruin a sale is to jump from one phase to another, and the best way to consistently make money is to pay attention and move clients through it in a logical way.

None of these are particularly complicated insights, but the fact of the matter is that most salespeople don't understand the sales process at all. They're "winging it" – not following any kind of systematic program to generate new sales – and, as a result, their production swings up and down from week to week and month to month. As a manager, you can help bring order and consistency by using a system and then reinforcing it. I've seen it again and again, in companies all over the world. MODERN isn't just a way to work, it's a plan of attack.

Sales systems are good for production, but they're also great management tools. Without one, managers tend to ask vague questions, such as "Did you get that sale? When do you think it will happen?" A system replaces that by offering a common language. You can ask better questions, like "Where are you in the sales process?" By working off of the same template, managers can also help their staff work through situations more efficiently.

Superstars are great, but don't become dependent on any one or two producers

18

Recently, I had the chance to visit with one of my best clients, a manufacturer of large equipment. Because I've worked with him a number of times, I've gotten to know his sales staff well. Their makeup is typical – a couple of producers making big money at the top, a few stragglers barely hanging on at the bottom, and a bunch of salespeople in the middle, making a few sales here and there without breaking into the top tier.

During our conversation, my client remarked how lucky he was that his two aces – one of whom was in his forties, the other nearly sixty – had stuck with the company. But I had to wonder, what would happen if his luck ran out? Together, the pair made up the lion's share of his revenue. If he lost either of them, the company would be faced with a huge challenge. If both of them left, it would be a disaster.

In short, he was never more than a phone call away from a very tough future. That's the problem with depending on a couple of top salespeople – they could leave at any time. Successful producers have a lot of ambition, and they make a lot of money. For those reasons, there is always the chance they might decide to retire, or start their own company. Or, because they're motivated by money, they might be lured away by a competitor who is willing to offer better terms. There's even the chance, however remote, they might leave for personal or medical reasons.

Don't be caught in that position. Appreciate your sales stars, but never forget you could lose them. Look past the top two or three producers, and be sure you're recruiting and training their replacements. You might luck out and have your best people stick around for a long time. But you don't want to be unprepared if they don't.

52 Things Every Sales Manager Needs to Know

How well do you really know your sales staff?

19

If you've read any of my books, or spent more than five minutes talking to me, then you probably already know that I'm a big proponent of scientific personality assessments. Part of the reason, of course, is that it can help you hire much stronger salespeople. But even if you already have a team in place, assessments can be a great way to take stock of what you have.

You shouldn't just stop with assessments, either. It's a very good idea to periodically spend a couple of hours with your team finding out how they're developing and where their relative strengths are. By investing a little bit of time in evaluation – in house or on the road with clients – you obtain useful information to get more out of your staff. Training, for instance, can be customized to address your group's weaker points. Or, you could offer guidance to individual producers who need it.

Another way you can use good knowledge about your sales team to your advantage is in matching them up with customers. By knowing their individual personality styles, along with their respective talents, you can send your salespeople where they're likely to find the greatest success. Or, in cases where this wouldn't be possible because of territories or seniority, you can at least help them prepare and anticipate where they're likely to face challenges.

52 Things Every Sales Manager Needs to Know

Low producers drain your energy, but most sales managers focus on them anyway

20

If you're spending most of your time with low producers – and most sales managers are – then you're probably using up a lot of your energy needlessly. That's because top performers, the superstar salespeople on your team, will almost always have a great personal attitude that lifts up your mood. In other words, they're great to be around, because they pick you up. Poor salespeople, however, tend to have the opposite effect. By constantly complaining and making excuses, they suck the energy and passion from the sales floor. Because of this, managers should be careful not to spend too much time with marginal salespeople.

A lot of managers would object to this line of thinking. Aren't low producers, after all, the ones who need the most help and guidance? Well, it really depends. That's because there are different kinds of low producers – the ones who aren't selling, and the ones who aren't selling yet.

The second group — the producers who just need experience or a new approach — aren't really low performers. They're actually trainees, and should get your time and attention. But the true low performers, the folks who haven't sold and aren't going to, aren't going to get much better no matter what you do for them. It's easy to tell the groups apart, because one brings excitement to their work, and the other doesn't.

Don't fall into the trap of spending all of your energy and effort at the bottom of the ladder. Coach those salespeople that want to learn and improve their craft, and don't worry about those who aren't interested. In time, they'll either catch on or be replaced by someone with a better attitude. And when that happens, you will feel better.

21

For me, the way a lot of companies run their sales training is a bit like a foreign game show – there's lots of hollering and excitement, but I can never figure out what they're trying to win. For example, several large firms I know send their sales team to a public motivational seminar each year. But despite the hundreds of dollars they spend on each ticket, they don't see any improvement. So finally, the same managers who have decided they don't have the time or budget to hire someone like me decide training doesn't work. My question is – how would they know?

Just to be clear, I don't have anything against public seminars. They can be a great way to give a shot of motivation. What I do have a problem with, however, is uncommitted managers trying to use them as a replacement for real training. Everything about the situation – from the generic approach to the annual timing – goes against the concept of continuous improvement. It's hard to overstate how much better off these companies would be with a real commitment to sales education.

Real training is focused; it's not something you do one time and leave in a conference room. It is truly a customized program that fits your organization and industry. If you do it correctly, you'll get gradual changes in behavior and performance instead of a two hour boost of enthusiasm. And that means repetition, hard work, and commitment from management and the sales team.

There isn't a shortcut or quick fix to training, so don't look for one. Treat it like an investment, not an expense, and it will pay you back like one.

A good mentor has already been where you want to be and can show you the way

22

Finding a good mentor and duplicating their success isn't exactly new advice, from me or any other successful business person. It deserves mention in this book, however, because it's an area that lots of managers overlook. It's only natural, given that most managers are experienced salespeople themselves. They've worked hard to climb up through the ranks, and now they find themselves mentoring others.

Just because you've made your way into a leadership role, however, doesn't mean you should stop looking for guidance along the way. You might be a veteran in sales, but new to management. You could lack expertise in an industry or geographic area. Or, you just might look for encouragement from time to time from someone who's been at it longer than you. There are lots of great reasons to have a mentor, and they're just as valid for managers as they are for salespeople.

So what should you look for in a mentor? A great candidate is anyone who likes you and has all the qualities you'll need to develop – a good attitude, a productive sales team, a great income, and maybe even a bigger title than you. Lots of sales managers go on to become corporate executives, and these people can show you how they made the jump. Ideally, you would look for someone within your company, as they might be more familiar with you and can be great contacts, but really they can be anyone who understands the profession.

Don't think just because you've moved on from the sales floor that you can't still use a mentor. You still have places to go, and there are always going to be people who got there first who can show the way.

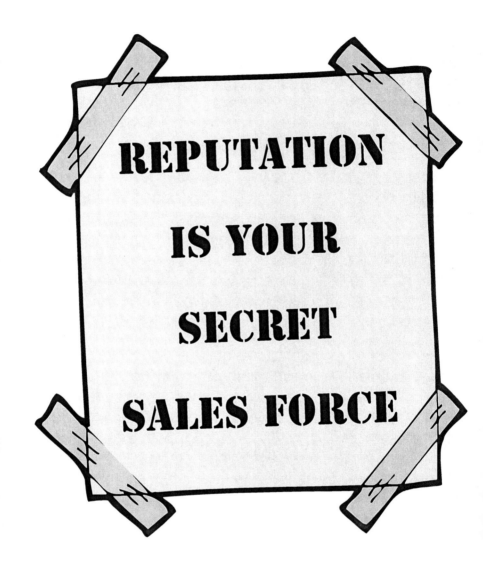

23

No matter how big your sales force is, chances are you wish you could have a couple more top performers – men and women who did nothing but generate more sales, and in a way that made you look great. Those superstars are closer than you think. In fact, you have dozens, hundreds or even thousands of them at your fingertips. Where are they hiding? In your customer list.

Satisfied clients can do more for your business – and your company's ongoing sales efforts – than anyone else you deal with. The way you mobilize them is by building up your reputation. In other words, if they have enough good things to say about you, you can be sure they will.

Building up a reputation isn't difficult, but it's not something you do overnight either. That's because a customer's faith in you doesn't usually come from one interaction, or even a few. Rather, it's the natural result of exceeding their expectations consistently. By going beyond the call of duty time and again, you allow them to gain a comfort with you that can grow and translate into absolute trust.

Remind your sales staff to look for ways to give that little bit of extra effort. Impress upon them that your reputation isn't an abstract idea, but something that will make sales easier and put money in their pockets. Make sure they understand that they have to do the right thing – both ethically and in terms of delivery – every single time. If you can accomplish that, you'll start to earn one reputation for service with your customers, and another for profits with your management.

Before you can graduate to big-time sales management, you must teach your staff the ABC's of selling

24

Early on in my career, I got a great tip from one of my first managers. He advised me that if I wanted to get ahead, I should learn my selling ABCs. It turned out to be good advice, and you can pass it on to your staff.

Basically there are three types of clients – A, B and C. "A" clients are best, the buyers that make up the bulk of your sales and keep your commission checks coming regularly. "B" clients are the next step down. They might not be ringing up huge sales for you, but they're still a dependable part of your business, with the potential to move up in the future. "C" customers, of course, are the marginal sales that come and go. You couldn't make a living selling to them, but there's always the chance they'll become stronger clients down the road.

Once you understand the three customer types, the trick is to correctly identify them and keep them moving through into a higher stage. One way is to keep selling up the food chain. If your producers currently have customers who are mid-level managers, then you could encourage them to look higher up in the company. Sometimes, time can take care of this for you. For example, several of the people I started working with early in my career have moved on to senior positions. As a result, our careers have grown together, allowing us to work at a higher level.

By always searching for "A" customers, and developing your other clients towards that point, you and your staff can spell out a great living.

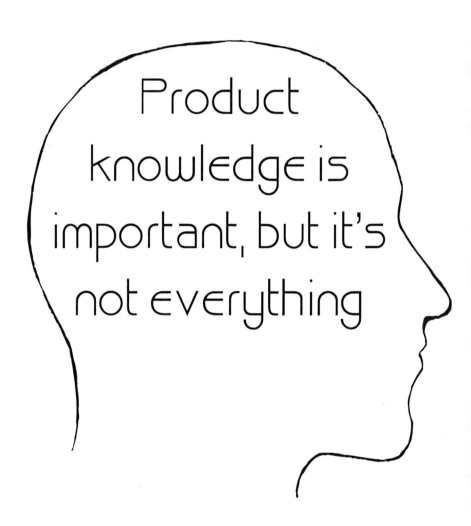

Among sales departments around the world, product knowledge is one of those core topics, similar to prospecting – just when it seems some managers aren't teaching it enough, others are emphasizing it too much. That's because, just like prospecting, product knowledge is important; it's just not the only thing that's important.

Let's be clear – your sales staff absolutely must know your solutions inside and out. Nothing will undermine their confidence faster than having to explain to a client why they can't answer basic questions about your widgets. Along those same lines, it helps if they know a little something about what the competitors are selling as well. So, as a manager you should be doing everything you can to be sure this happens. Sometimes this can be accomplished with meetings, brochures, or technical specs. Other times you might want to have someone from engineering or product development speak to your group to round out their understanding.

Realize, though, that there's a fine line between doing it and overdoing it. Product knowledge is important to your team's success – maybe 40% – but that still leaves another 60% that depends on their sales skills and execution. This means sales systems, closing and negotiating, qualifying, and yes, lots of prospecting.

The greatest salespeople have great product knowledge, but they don't sell on that alone. Make sure your producers have a well-rounded base of knowledge, and one that extends beyond your facilities and websites. It's one thing to know about everything you make or do, but it's another thing to be able to find customers and close deals.

BE A LEADER FIRST

1

AND A FRIEND SECOND

2

Being a manager isn't easy, especially if you've been promoted from the sales floor. Being put in charge places a barrier between yourself and the other producers you worked beside day after day, sometimes for years.

Some take the transition well, while others need more time to adjust. The best way to speed the process along is to remember what you're there for – to help your team make more sales. Often, this means you can't be a best friend the way you were in the past. As hard as this will be, the best thing is to get over it and make new friends. You need to run your staff like a leader, and you won't be able to do it if they think of you as an old buddy.

With that in mind, be friendly to the sales staff. Let them know you're still the same person, but you now have a different job, and one that requires you to deal with them in a different way. It's alright to go out for dinner and a drink once in a while, but don't make a habit of blending in too much. There will come a day when you'll have to discipline someone, or give a less than stellar performance review. That will be a lot easier if you seem more like a boss, and less like a buddy. Acting like a manager might cost you some friendships, but it will gain you the trust and respect of your staff.

52 Things Every Sales Manager Needs to Know

A great sales manager can see through walls

27

No sales department, regardless of how talented, experienced, or driven they might be, can achieve superstar numbers by themselves. Business is a team sport, and top managers know they have to work with other departments in their companies if they want to generate great sales numbers.

Besides, integrating your team with other parts of the organization doesn't have to be difficult. Reach out to managers in the shipping, accounting or product development departments, as well as any others that play a major role in your company or industry. Explain to them that you want your sales staff to know what goes on throughout the rest of the company. See if you can arrange a quick tour or a shared meeting once in a while. You'd be amazed at what the small gesture can do for you and your staff.

Almost immediately, it gives your sales team more ammunition to close business in the field. Having a working knowledge of what goes on past their own offices enhances confidence and product understanding. At the same time, it encourages cooperation and makes other departments more sympathetic to your cause. Instead of being a name on the other end of an e-mail or phone call, they see the sales staff as colleagues. That kind of teamwork comes in handy when you need technical details or an expedited request. And while you're at it, make sure that you go up the chain of command as well. Let senior management know how hard your group works, and what they could use to bring in even more business.

Great sales managers aren't just supervisors, they're also connectors. Bring together all the parts of your company, help to build a sales-focused organization, and you won't have to wait long for the payoff.

A resume never sold anything

28

If you're a fan of sports, you might have seen some of the various drafts that the professional leagues run each year to choose their future star players. If you haven't, it's basically just as you remember from the playground. The teams with the first picks select the biggest and strongest kids, on down the line until everybody has been picked.

The amazing thing is, even with months to prepare and millions of dollars at stake, lots of draft picks fail. In some cases, scouts and coaches spend weeks and months agonizing over whom to take, and still get it wrong. In many cases the player just doesn't turn out to be as good as advertised, and often they don't even stay on the team. Now, compare this once-a-year ritual to the way most sales managers bring in fresh faces. Is it any wonder most new salespeople don't work out?

Most sales managers are like those draft day scouts, so distracted by facts and figures (in this case a resume) that they don't look at the underlying person. They decide certain candidates are winners based on a grade point average or successful sports background, and don't investigate any further. Even forgetting that something like 70% of people lie on their resume, this is a poor policy because it could allow you to miss out on potential superstars who have the drive to succeed, but not the paper background you think you need.

If you want to hire effectively, weigh resumes with other information available, like their interviewing skills, and especially sales personality assessments. You won't always get the flashiest people, but you'll get the right ones for your sales team.

If you only talk with your staff at the annual sales meeting, you have a communication problem

29

Through my speaking and seminar business, I have the opportunity to attend dozens of sales meetings every year. For the most part, they're pretty similar – awards are given, speeches are made, and everybody gets a nice meal. But beyond the usual fanfare, these gatherings are revealing. By simply watching how managers interact with their sales staff, I'm able to tell quite a bit about how well they're doing.

The best supervisors use the time to congratulate their sales team and relay some goals for the coming year. The sloppy managers have a harder job. Instead of looking ahead, they're still catching up on the past year. Unsure of what their salespeople have been up to, they're forced to make guesses about what sort of targets to set, or which areas to work on. In each case, they could have made their lives a lot easier by keeping better tabs week to week.

This isn't to say that you should smother your salespeople. You should always want and be working towards having your team be as self-sufficient as possible. But too many managers take this concept too far. Abandoning your staff doesn't do them any favors. Your job shouldn't be to micromanage, but you do still need to guide things along.

This all points to constant communication. You want a real sense of what's going on in your office and your territory. Don't ask your salespeople "how things are going." Instead, get specific feedback about their activity, their clients, or where they are in the sales process. Doing so will force both you and your salespeople to think about how things are going, along with areas of possible improvement.

Business phrases are like fashion styles: they come and go each year, but the classic ideas seem to return, in one shape or another, again and again. So it doesn't surprise me that so much has been made recently about CRM – Customer Relationship Management.

At its core, the idea isn't that new: devise ways to take better care of your customers and, chances are, business will grow. What makes the latest incarnation different is the idea that companies can use software and database systems. While I'm probably not the best person to advise you on the ins and outs of computerizing your company, I can tell you that almost any sales department can benefit from taking this philosophy and tying it together with the use of a strong sales system.

When I first began teaching The MODERN Sales System, I tried to emphasize that the magic wasn't in the letters themselves, but the action guides that made the system work. By mastering those, any salesperson could become a top performer, but doing so took a great deal of practice and organization.

Modern software programs, however, have made this process much smoother. By implementing the steps into a contact manager or database, salespeople can easily glimpse where their customers are in the sales process. Even better, they can share that information with their managers.

By keeping those sorts of reminders at their fingertips, a good sales system becomes that much more usable and effective. Not every trend is worth following, but CRM can help you and your staff by reminding you to do the things you should.

Cutting your price, even by a small percentage, will eventually put you out of business

31

It's amazing how often businesses in general, and especially sales departments, sink their own future by offering discounts. Often, they don't even realize they're doing it. Like the proverbial "death by a thousand cuts," no small concession is fatal, but, put together, they create a situation in which things can only get worse.

The reason for a price cut is always simple – to generate more sales. Someone in the organization, whether it's the president, the head of the manufacturing department or just a nervous salesperson, decides to give up a bit of their margin to make things easier.

Everything that happens after that moment, however, conspires to doom the salesperson, the company, and everyone else on their side of the table. To begin with, the price cut represents a loss of money. There are now fewer funds available for research, training, maintenance and other operating expenses, not to mention a smaller commission on the sale.

At the same time, both the customer and the salesperson learn a sticky lesson: that it's easier to close new business by cutting prices. What happens the next time the customer buys? Do they ask for the old price? Of course not! They've learned they can hold out for a discount. And don't forget the salesperson. They've become conditioned to think the easiest way out of the tension of negotiation is to give discounts.

For these reasons, sales managers should do everything in their power to hold tight on margins. Emphasize building value in meetings; when you go on sales calls with your team, resist the urge to cave on prices. If they see you have to cut prices to make a sale, that will speak volumes about what you think of your own products and prices.

It only takes one

to bring down your whole team

32

Sales isn't an easy field. To succeed over time you need to have a good attitude, because it's the only thing that will keep you going during the hard times. As a manager, you've probably already noticed how important it is to stay positive in your own career. And hopefully, you remind your sales staff to keep their heads and spirits up as well.

But what about those salespeople on your staff who have a bad attitude, the ones who always seem to be grumbling and complaining? Most times, managers just hang on to them, thinking that's just "the way it is" with that person. So long as they sell, the rationale goes, they're doing more good than harm.

The reality, however, is that they're bad for morale. Moaning and groaning, or a lack of cooperation, brings down your entire staff and inject a pessimistic tone. Even worse is sending one of these people out into the field. Most managers tend to think of a bad apple in terms of what happens between their own walls, but what do they think happens when they meet with clients? Do they become bundles of sunshine then? Of course not. They continue complaining – about you, your company, your products, and so on.

If you have a bad attitude in your staff, you have to decide whether it's worth it to keep such people. Are they acting out for some specific reason? Are they even aware that they're doing it? Sometimes, a private talk or a few reminders can correct the behavior. But for most of them, things will never change. In those cases, it's better to cut them loose. Keeping them around will only drain your energy. And besides, with a bad attitude, it's unlikely that they're going to become sales superstars anyway.

Keep meetings short and to the point

33

A top producer working for one of my best clients recently told me that she hates to go into the office. When I asked why, she answered that her manager liked to hold long, pointless meetings, and that her time was better spent in the field. I've heard this sentiment echoed again and again over the years, to the point where I'm forced to wonder why supervisors are holding so many meetings in the first place.

The first step to cutting back on meeting fatigue is reducing the number that you have. How many times do you get together with your salespeople each month? What would happen if you cut that number in half? If the answer is "nothing too bad," give it a try. This isn't to say that you shouldn't have regular sales meetings. Communicating with your staff, and getting feedback from them, is one of a manager's most important roles. But that doesn't mean you should tie up your entire sales team for hours a week with nothing important to say.

Once you've cut back on the number of meetings, try to trim their length as well. Have a set time, and a firm agenda. Resist the urge to stray off-topic, unless the material is critical. If you, or someone on your staff, have something urgent to say, say it. Otherwise, mark it down to follow up on a different day. Doing so will force you to think about what's important and focus your time accordingly.

Sales meetings are an important part of a manager's job, but you should never hold them just for the sake of getting together. Your sales staff is busy, and you should be too. Use your time to make your team stronger and you might notice a side effect – your salespeople will actually want to show up.

52 Things Every Sales Manager Needs to Know

A great manager knows the cost of a hiring mistake

34

You've probably heard or read that a company, on average, loses three times the salary of a hiring mistake. That's a pretty scary number, if you ever take the time to think about it, especially when you consider how few sales hires work out. To make matters worse, I think it might actually be a bit low when it comes to sales staff.

Consider for a moment everything that goes into bringing a new producer into your company. First, there are the interviewing costs themselves. In order to find candidates, you might have to pay for an ad in a paper, or a booth at a job fair. From there, you're forced to take hours and hours of your own time digging through resumes and arranging interview times, to say nothing of the actual hours spent personally with the top prospects. Assuming you're worth your salary, those figures can be extreme. Don't forget the costs of background checks and personality assessments. And, in some cases, you can add airfare, hotel, and other travel expenses on top.

Then, of course, there are the training costs, which can go on for weeks while a territory sits idle and no new clients are served. But all of these ignore the biggest expenses of all – the wear and tear a bad hire puts on your customers and other sales staff. Often, it's months or longer before you know whether your new hire will pan out. During that time, the wrong person can bring down morale in the office and alienate your customers in the field, all of which makes it even harder for the next person to succeed. When you're looking for staff, choose carefully. Hiring mistakes are expensive, and chances are you won't ever know just how much the wrong person has cost you.

NEVER ASK YOUR SALESPEOPLE TO DO SOMETHING YOU CAN'T OR WON'T DO YOURSELF

35

To get the most out of their sales team, every manager needs at least two things: respect and credibility. In many cases, these come naturally from the manager's own successful career. The staff knows the manager can walk the walk, and so they listen to what's being said and taught. But whether managers are superstar salespeople, or if they've never sold a thing, nothing takes away their standing faster than asking their staff to do something they can't or won't do themselves.

Sometimes this shows itself in unrealistic demands, as with the manager who asks each member of his team to make a hundred cold calls each day, even though he's never made one himself. Other times, it's a lack of competence. For instance, the manager preaches the value of holding firm on price margins, but constantly gives away discounts in the field. No matter what the specific cause, the effect is always the same – the manager must work in a diminished capacity.

Salespeople no longer come to the manager for help. And why should they, if they know they'll just be asked to do something unreasonable, or given advice that isn't practical? In short, the manager becomes an obstacle to the sale, not a resource in closing it.

Keep your credibility in mind when dealing with your staff. Don't set goals you know they can't meet, or ask them to perform in a way that you know isn't feasible. You might think you're motivating them, but what you're really doing is setting the conditions for them to tune you out. Remember, being an effective manager is all about good leadership, and great leaders aren't just followed for what they say, it's what they do that counts.

Superior sales managers need to be superior presenters

To become a great manager means becoming a great leader. And you can't accomplish that without strong presentation skills. It's simply not possible to inspire others if you can't convey your message to them, whether it's a motivational pep talk, or just a bit of product knowledge. Yet, as I've met managers around the world, I'm surprised time and again to see how many of them are poor presenters, and how few of them are working on it.

I think some of their lack of effort can be explained by the way we think about public speaking. There is a perception that some of us are "born with it," and if you aren't one of them, you can never learn to be a strong presenter. I can tell you from personal experience that this is simply not true. Any of us, by learning the fundamentals of effective communication, can learn to be much stronger.

Good presentation skills are so important that I devoted the final third of my book, The MODERN Sales System, to ways to learn and hone them. If your talks lack the firepower they need, that might be a good place to start. Other ways to improve include books, seminars, coaching, toastmasters clubs, and, of course, practice. When it comes to improving your speaking skills, or just about any other skills, for that matter, nothing beats repetition.

There's a reason fiery speeches are a staple of sports movies and successful political campaigns. It's human nature for us to want to follow the people who can inspire us with their words. Take advantage of that power. You don't have to give legendary keynotes to be effective; all it takes is a little work and practice.

Never stop recruiting superstars

A major mistake that lots of sales managers make is waiting until a job needs to be filled. When one of their salespeople leaves, they suddenly find themselves with an empty desk and an unserviced territory. So, they go out looking for warm bodies in a mad rush. Soon, they find three or four people. They might not be great candidates, but they can start right away, and so they're brought on. Predictably, most of them don't work out, and the manager ends up back where he or she started.

Wiser managers, however, keep prospecting for salespeople on an ongoing basis. They attend college fairs, run ads, and remind their staff to keep their eyes open. Even when they don't have any openings, they keep looking. They know that finding great salespeople is a lot like prospecting for new clients – it's always easier to find someone when you don't need them, and you can never have too many great leads in the pipeline. Then, when an opportunity comes along, they have a file full of great people.

Some managers will even go as far as to hire a great prospect even if they don't have a place for them. They simply mentor them and wait, knowing people come and go and that a territory will open up sooner or later. This might seem a bit extreme, to have someone on the payroll without a place, but I think it's a much smarter strategy than hiring someone out of frustration or desperation. When you hire out of panic, you usually get it wrong. By hurrying the process, you throw away sales and new customers.

Treat your sales staff like you would a client list; find someone great, and then start looking again. There's always someone great out there, and the worst time to look is when you need them the most.

Track activity, because results will always follow

I can remember a scene from my early days in sales that I'm sure plays itself out in countless offices around the world every day. My manager, a former salesperson himself, emerged from his office into the morning meeting to announce that the quarter was about to close and he wanted a couple new sales from everyone. From where, I wondered, did he think these magical sales were going to fall? In real estate, like most businesses, a successful close is the result of weeks or possibly months of hard work. Pulling one out of thin air just wasn't feasible.

My manager would have been better off had he made his announcement months ahead of time. And, in any case, he was missing the point. Rather than focusing on sales, he should have been concentrating on activity. At first glance, this might not seem to make sense. After all, as salespeople, we get paid to close, not to make calls. But that thinking comes from a skewed perspective, and here's why: we can't control how many sales we make directly, nor can we force anyone to buy or say for certain which deals will close, but we can choose to make enough calls or set enough appointments to guarantee we'll hit our goals.

As trite as it might seem, sales is still a numbers game. Get a certain number of referrals, and you're bound to get a new customer. Make enough calls, and you're bound to get a few leads out of them. The ratios might not hold up day to day, and you might improve on them with training, but over time your performance is very highly predicted by the amount of effort you put in. Smart managers recognize this and look for activity from their sales staff, because they know the results are bound to follow.

Make sure your sales team knows their value proposition

Watch any television program and you're going to learn something interesting about sales. All kinds of businesses, from major corporations to local car dealers, spend millions each year to tell you all about their value propositions – ten or fifteen second descriptions of what they do and how they can help you. The messages might be hidden behind pretty people, quick camera cuts and upbeat music, but they're always there.

Your sales staff should know their value propositions, because there are customers around every corner, and sometimes you only get a few seconds to grab their attention. In some circles, this is called an "elevator speech." I'm not a huge fan of this term, since the word "speech" implies that you should bore every stranger with the details of your career. But even so, every salesperson is going to find themselves in social and business situations where they're asked about their work.

Good managers make sure their team both has and uses a strong value proposition. In some cases, you might want to suggest a few ways to word things in a way that will catch the attention of the right prospect. It's important they sound natural coming out of the salesperson's mouth. For instance, mine is "I help companies immediately improve their sales, margins and customer service." Could I say it differently? Sure, but this way reflects my style. Practice with your staff until each of them can explain the benefits of working with you in a way that works for them. Your producers are going to meet hundreds or thousands of people each year. Make sure they know and can explain what you stand for, and you'll see those contacts coming back as customers.

EXCEED THE EXPECTATIONS OF ALL OF YOUR CUSTOMERS, WHETHER THEY'RE INSIDE OR OUTSIDE YOUR WALLS

Why is it that so many companies treat their employees like second-class citizens? I suppose it's human nature to take people for granted. In other words, they see the external customer as a chance for new or continued revenue, where the employee is another person on the payroll.

This is such a prevalent and disastrous attitude that I devoted a portion of my book, The PEOPLE Approach to Customer Service, to resolving it. As a sales manager, you must ensure that other departments are being treated by your staff as well as they would be if they were clients. To do any less is inviting trouble. That's because the chain of contact doesn't end at your office, or on the other end of the phone. You're always either serving a customer or working with someone who is.

To that end, try to set the tempo yourself. Make sure your sales staff understands that sales-driven organizations – those that bring in the most business and the greatest incomes – work as a two-way street. On the one hand, they should want and expect other departments and personnel to do whatever they can to support the sales staff. On the other hand, it's the responsibility of the sales department to make that as easy as possible by giving everyone else in the company the tools and respect they need to pitch in.

52 Things Every Sales Manager Needs to Know

The best thing you can do for your staff is to make them strong in the basics

41

When I took my first sales job, fresh out of college, I realized something valuable – that I didn't know anything about selling. Realizing that I was about to jump into the battle of commission sales unarmed, I started taking in anything I thought might be able to help with the fight. I consumed books, magazines and seminars, treating each one the same way as I had my coursework only weeks before.

Luckily, my first two bosses, Matt and Don Terrace, were committed to helping me figure things out. Each day working for them was like a taste of boot camp. The morning meeting brought questions about the sales process, methods for overcoming common objections, and demonstrations of basic sales techniques. As the weeks went by, my colleagues and I began to absorb the lessons through sheer repetition, until we were able to move through each phase of the sale effortlessly.

I didn't know it then, but the two of them weren't just setting the stage for my success, but for their own as well. By ensuring that every single salesperson on their staff was strong in the basics, they made it possible for us to master more advanced techniques later. In other words, they were laying a strong foundation that could be built upon in the future. We were always going to sell, and our closing ratios would only improve over time.

The lesson that I want to leave you with is simple: make sure your salespeople are strong in the basics, especially when they're new. I've never met anyone with a degree in sales, and most of us don't come into this industry knowing exactly what it's about. Take the time to teach them what they need to know. They'll get a bit of confidence, and you'll get peace of mind.

PROSPECTING IS THE LIFEBLOOD OF ANY SALES DEPARTMENT

42

No matter what business you're in, it's highly unlikely that your sales come out of nowhere. Put another way, there are very few products that actually "sell themselves," and it's a rare situation where prospective customers trip over each other in a mad rush to get their money in your hands. And yet, many salespeople, and managers, act like they expect that very thing to happen. Instead of prospecting and continually bringing new business to the door, they fixate on existing clients or a few good leads, effectively betting their pay on one good outcome.

Most of the time, this is a losing strategy. Even the best clients can leave, retire, or switch vendors. The strongest prospects can change their mind or lose their budget. The only way to be sure of making a sale is to have lots of potential customers moving through the pipeline.

If your team isn't filling and working their sales funnel, constantly finding new contacts and churning them through the sales process, then it's your job to set them on the right path. Be sure they know and understand the value of finding fresh faces and act accordingly. Take a few minutes each week to meet with them individually and talk about whom they're working with, where they're finding potential customers, and how they can move them through the funnel with less time and resistance.

New customers don't come from nowhere, and neither does an attitude of continuous prospecting. It's up to the manager to set the tone. Teach your sales staff to prospect continuously and the sales funnel won't just give you leads, it will give you consistency.

Make sure everyone on your staff knows you're there to serve the client

43

For all that I've said and believe about prospecting, I'd still rather have five happy customers than ten good prospects. It's just good common sense; the people most likely to buy from you in the future are the ones who already made the decision to do so in the past. They already know all about you and your products, so unless you've treated them poorly, you should have an easier time going forward than you did making the first sale.

There are also economics at work. As any astute manager could tell you, it costs several times more to bring in a new customer than it does to service an existing one. In many industries, leads generated through print ads, online campaigns and other media come at a steep price – often hundreds or thousands of dollars per qualified contact. Factor in the salesperson's time and travel, along with the fact that new customers tend to place smaller orders, and you can easily see how the math works against you.

So what should all of this mean to you as a manager? It means that you should be doing everything you can to instill an attitude of customer satisfaction in your team. Be sure they understand where their paychecks are coming from, and where they are likely to keep coming from in the future. Ask them about prospects and sales funnels, but don't stop there. Make sure they're checking in with existing customers and keeping them happy. If one of your salespeople has a customer who moves or leaves his or her company, be sure they keep in touch. A buyer at one organization is likely to end up in a similar job somewhere else. At the end of the day, the only thing better than making a sale is making another one, and everyone on your staff should know the easiest way to do that.

44

For most of this book, I've made a point of showing how managers who are involved can help their salespeople reach new levels. But that philosophy can only be taken so far. Eventually, you have to step back and let them succeed – and sometimes fail – on their own.

The line between helping and stifling is a fine one, but I think it's best to err on the side of letting your staff take a few bruises. Why? Because there's no better teacher than failure. No matter who taught you to ride a bike, and however sharp their guidance and encouragement was, chances are you had to fall a couple of times before you got the hang of it. It's no different learning to sell. Every manager should be competent enough, and willing enough, to show any member of their team how to prospect, qualify, negotiate and close a prospect. But after you've done so, take a backseat.

In the field, this can be harder than it sounds. When you're meeting with a prospect, the temptation is to jump in and correct mistakes immediately, especially when you see the sale slipping away. But unless it's a situation that can't be salvaged or a major client that can't be sacrificed, my advice would be to let the salesperson work. You can always debrief and offer advice after the fact, and taking control of the sale away from them during the client is only going to hurt their confidence and credibility.

As a sales manager, you should be able to do everything you ask your salespeople to do. At the same time, if you want them to grow into the kind of team you'll want to manage, you'll need the patience to only do it once in a while.

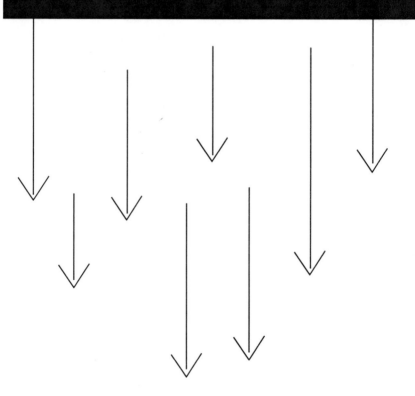

45

In case you missed out on the memo, sales management isn't easy. While I've focused most of my attention on working with your sales staff – the meat and potatoes part of a manager's job – the fact is that there's often as much work to do above the food chain as there is below. That's because no sales department works in a vacuum. CEO's, corporate boards and other senior management types all have ideas about what your group should be doing, regardless of whether they've ever sold anything themselves.

At different times, it's probable that one or more of these groups will impose demands on you or your team. In some cases, they might ask you to move a certain product before it becomes unmarketable. Or, they could ask that you look to promote service plans that are part of the company's new focus area. Sometimes they might just ask you to "sell more" to keep the books in good shape. But no matter what the request is, be very careful about how you translate those requests to your team.

Your salespeople should already be busy. Consider whether the new requests make sense and are feasible to put into action. If they fail on either count , if they don't fit in with your organization's other long-term plans, or if they would be impossible to carry out, take those issues up with the person or group asking, rather than passing them on below. Asking your staff to do the impossible is an easy way to lose their trust and credibility. It's better to have a frank discussion on the front end about what does make sense and can be done then it is to agree to a bad idea.

52 Things Every Sales Manager Needs to Know

Start a LIBRARY for your sales team

46

What if you could have an expert on sales come into your office and give an all day presentation for less than you'd spend on a tank of gas? Well, the good news is that you can – you just have to buy a book.

Every year, publishers release hundreds of titles on selling, not to mention other topics like negotiation, goal-setting, and even management. Why not have a few of them available for yourself and your sales team? Not only will it probably be the cheapest investment you'll ever have to make in your team's training, but it might pay surprising dividends. Even if you, along with each member of your staff, only read one book per month, you'd bring hundreds of new ideas into your office each year. What's more, it wouldn't take any of you more than a few minutes each day.

Starting your library doesn't have to involve anything expensive or complicated. Simply clear a shelf somewhere and bring in a couple of the classics on sales. You should be able to think of a few on your own, but if you need a little bit of guidance, simply send me an e-mail and I'll be happy to point you towards a few titles to get started. From there, read a couple of them and encourage your team to do the same. Ask them what they thought or learned, and what kinds of books they'd like to see you add in the future. Once they're in the habit of reading a few minutes each day, you might even throw some CD's or magazines into the mix.

In every strong sales department I've worked with over the years, there is one thing that's always common: they all have an attitude of continuous learning. And while seminars and training are an important part of that, nothing beats a little bit of reading to fill in the gaps.

Teach your salespeople time management and goal setting — they're the backbones of a successful selling career

In all likelihood, you've gotten to where you are by having strong time management and goal-setting skills. To get to where you'd like to be next – a successful manager with big pay and lots of free time – you've got to teach them to your staff.

It would be difficult, if not impossible, to have a great career in sales without being able to manage the salesperson's two most valuable commodities: time and energy. Even so, most of us have never taken a time management course, and I meet lots of salespeople who haven't even written down their daily, monthly or yearly targets. As a result, they aren't moving towards anything; they're just floating around in space hoping to come across a sale.

For example, I see lots of salespeople set two appointments: one at ten o'clock, and the other at three in the afternoon. They spend the morning preparing for the first appointment, and then the four hours in between waiting for the second. You can see the same thing in salespeople that go on the road Monday afternoon and return on Thursday. They use up the better part of their week traveling and adjusting, when they could be selling.

Of course, managing time is important, but it takes a backseat to setting strong targets and reaching them. After all, as the old saying goes, "without goals, you don't have a time management problem." In other words, if you don't know what you're aiming for, it doesn't really matter how long it takes you to achieve it. Goals create energy, and time management allows us to use it. Instill a strong sense of both in your staff, because without them, none of you will ever break through and become superstars.

48

A few years ago, a small company in Seattle's Pikes Place Fish Market made big waves in the business world. Their revolution was unique because they didn't look for ways to boost revenue, cut staff costs or engage in some kind of marketing push, although they accomplished all of these things. No, the secret to their success was much simpler – they decided to have fun.

Just by having a good time, the management found that employees worked harder, profits went up, and customers were happier. This shouldn't come as a surprise. When we're having fun, we tend to make a lot more money, especially in sales. Lighter moods breed confidence and creativity, while tension makes it harder to break free and come up with innovative solutions. In short, happier work is better work. And besides, who wants to work in an office that's uptight anyway?

What's the easiest way to bring a bit of joy to your sales team? The first step is to have a good time yourself. Set the pace by relaxing a little. Get your work done, but don't be afraid to crack a smile or have a laugh now and then. Just as importantly, keep the atmosphere around your office light; don't let anyone be afraid to make a mistake. Fear is a big damper on fun and creativity, so take it as far away from the equation as possible.

Most successful people didn't get that way because they hate what they're doing. Try to have a good time and encourage your staff to do the same. Work actually can be fun – especially when you're making a ton of sales.

Show me the values you reward and I will show you the behavior you will receive

Think back to your days as a young child. How did your parents teach and reward you? If you're like most of us, a clean room got you an allowance. Maybe a good report card was worth an ice cream cone, or it could be that you were given a new toy for doing the dishes each week.

What you did or what you got doesn't matter. The point is that your parents had things they wanted you to do, and some reward that reinforced that behavior. Over time, you realized they would always look at your grades or the state of your room, and you could help yourself by making an effort to earn those rewards. Now think about your sales staff. What behaviors are you reinforcing? What actions do you notice and track? Are they the same ones that you say are important?

If you're honest in your assessment, you might find that your messages aren't as congruent as you think. For instance, one of my clients emphasized to me (and his staff) again and again that selling at high margins was the highest priority. Every training brochure and video, every advertisement, spoke to this need for price integrity as an overriding concern. And yet, when I visited their sales floor, the first thing I saw was a board showing each salesperson's gross sales. Moreover, the sales manager routinely gave price cuts to move volume and gave bonuses based on which member of his team could empty the most inventory. "Margins" might have been the buzzword, but "volume" was the real message.

Pavlov might not have been training salespeople with his infamous bells, but he could have been. Learn from his principles and tell your sales staff what you want, and then reinforce it with action. The sales floor is no place for mixed messages.

Learn how to spot a **slump,** and how to break one

50

Sales is like any other business – it definitely has its ups and downs. Through the years, I've found that with hard work and a good attitude, you can stay on the "up" most of the time, and when you are, things are great; sales pour in, customers seem to close themselves, and the paychecks are thick. When you're on a roll in sales, even the food seems to taste better.

The other side of the coin, though, can be rough. When you're not selling, everything is hard; prospecting feels like a chore, referrals dodge your calls, and even your best clients can't or won't buy. Sometimes, the slump is a result of forces beyond your control – a bad economy, problems in the company, or trouble from a competitor. Often, though, you find yourself unable to make the big sales because you're in a rut. You lose the passion for what your doing and customers pick up on it. To sell like a star means bringing passion and energy; you can't get there by going through the motions.

So how do we break free and start selling again? I've found that the best way is to do things differently. What form different takes isn't really the point, only that you get out of your own comfort zone a bit. Question everything you do, and see how far you can go towards putting new ideas in your head. Maybe you can read some new material or visit a different part of your company. Prospect in a different way or demonstrate a new product. You could even try eating at a new restaurant or driving to work on a different route. More often than not, it isn't our industry or the economy that needs a jolt, it's our imaginations. Open yourself up a bit and you might find that your slump will melt away with a change of routine.

Don't pay so much attention to taking care of your work that you forget to take care of yourself

51

There's a growing trend in today's world – especially amongst managers and executives – toward more and more work, and less and less attention to our own well-being. In other words, most of us put the care of our companies, our careers, and our employees above concern for ourselves. And while our generation certainly didn't invent this problem, we'd do well to improve on things if we want to get the most out of our lives.

This isn't just good personal advice. Studies have repeatedly shown that things like exercise, good nutrition, and getting the proper amount of rest can make a huge difference in your job performance. It turns out that being healthy doesn't just make you look better and live longer – it also makes you smarter, faster, and more creative. Besides, when you're taking care of yourself, it's easier for your staff to have more respect for you. By being seen as healthy and vibrant, you increase the odds they'll listen to your instructions and advice.

As with most things, it's really good habits that keep you in good shape. If you've been away from the treadmill for a while, or if you've forgotten where the vegetable aisle sits, start small. Get up fifteen minutes early and take a walk around the block. Decide to skip the late night television and go to bed half an hour earlier. Or, decide to have a salad for lunch a couple of times a week. Neither is going to make you into an Olympian overnight, but they can get the ball rolling so you can take on a more ambitious program.

Treat your body and mind at least as well as you would someone who works for you, because you're going to have to rely on them for a long time.

52 Things Every Sales Manager Needs to Know

Throughout this book, I've been throwing out many of my best management tips. Some of them relate directly to sales, while others are just points for strong leadership. As a great sales manager, you're going to need both. But, before you jump back out into the world, let me give you one last tool, the secret weapon in the sales manager's arsenal: listening.

Think back to your selling days. When were the sales really made, the deals really closed? When the prospect told you what they needed, and why. You may have moved to the corner office, but guess what? Nothing has changed. Listening is still the best way to find out what's happening. Listen long enough, and people will tell you everything: what's going on with your staff, what customers are buying, where your company and industry are headed, and so on.

If you want to speed that process along, learn to ask good questions. Go beyond generic inquiries and find out where the real challenges and opportunities lie. No manager ever made a breakthrough or inspired their team by asking "did you make any sales today?" Trade those kinds of questions for the more specific. Ask your team how many leads they generated, where a client is in the sales process, or how they feel they are handling objections, price challenges, etc. It might take more time and attention, but you're going to find out things you can't any other way.

There is a lot to being a sales manager. Some of it is technical and scientific, but most of it just comes down to leading people. Get it right and they'll follow you, but you have to know what's going on around you – and you can't do that without putting an ear to the ground once in a while.

Carl Henry is a sales educator, keynote speaker and corporate consultant. During the course of his own successful career, he developed The MODERN Sales System, which he has been sharing with companies and associations around the world for many years.

A Certified Speaking Professional and a member of the National Speakers Association, Carl teaches essential sales skills with humor, insight and personal experience. Hundreds of companies throughout a diverse range of industries have used his highly-acclaimed seminars to educate and inspire their sales teams.

Carl's other books include The MODERN Sales System, The PEOPLE Approach to Customer Service and 15 Hot Tips that Will Supercharge Your Sales Career.

He currently lives in Charlotte, North Carolina.

To order additional copies of this book, or find out about Carl's seminars contact him at:

Henry Associates
704-847-7390
9430 Valley RoadCharlotte, NC 28270
chenry@carlhenry.com
www.carlhenry.com

Printed in the United States
203934BV00006B/1-54/P